Copyright © 2015 Hallmark Licensing, LLC
Published by Hallmark Gift Books,
a division of Hallmark Cards, Inc.,
Kansas City, MO 64141
Visit us on the Web at Hallmark.com.

Editorial Director: Carrie Bolin
Editor: Lindsay Evans
Art Director: Jan Mastin
Designer: Brian Pilachowski
Production Designer: Dan Horton

ISBN: 978-1-59530-755-2
1BOK2204

Printed and bound in China

A Gift For:

_____

From:

_____

I'm Here for You

BY Ellen Brenneman

Hallmark

We can't know why the li

s so brief a time to *bloom*...

. . . in the warmth of

sunlight's kiss

upon its face . . .

. . . before it *folds* its fragrance in . . .

. . . and bids the world

good night . . .

. . . to rest its *beaut*

a gentler place.

But we can know that nothing
that is *loved* is ever lost,

. . . and no one who has ev

uched a *heart*
can really pass away,

. . . because some *beauty* lingers on . . .

. . . in each *memory*

of which they've been a part.

If you have enjoyed this book
or it has touched your life in some way,
we would love to hear from you.

Please send your comments to:

Hallmark Book Feedback

P.O. Box 419034

Mail Drop 100

Kansas City, MO 64141

Or e-mail us at:

booknotes@hallmark.com